AF088876

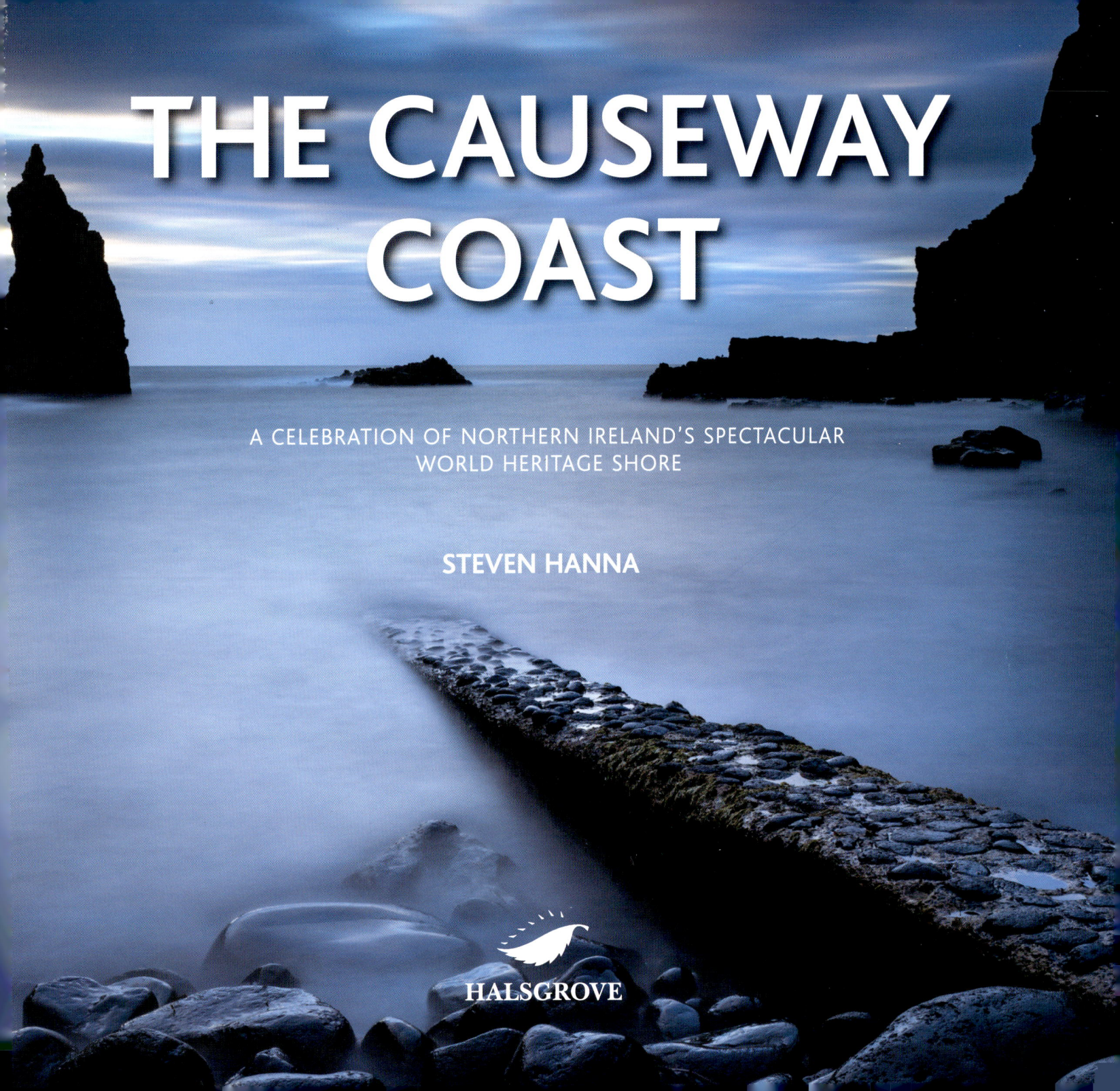

First published in Great Britain in 2017

Copyright © Steven Hanna 2017

All rights reserved. No part of this publication may be reproduced, stored in a retrieval system, or transmitted in any form or by any means without the prior permission of the copyright holder

British Library Cataloguing-in-Publication Data
A CIP record for this title is available from the British Library

ISBN 978 0 85704 304 7

HALSGROVE
Halsgrove House,
Ryelands Business Park,
Bagley Road, Wellington, Somerset TA21 9PZ
Tel: 01823 653777   Fax: 01823 216796
email: sales@halsgrove.com

Part of the Halsgrove group of companies
Information on all Halsgrove titles is available at: www.halsgrove.com

Printed and bound by Parksons Graphics, India

Portstewart, Co. Londonderry

INTRODUCTION

Rugged. Dramatic. Epic.

I'm asked many times how I would describe the Causeway Coast. Several words come to mind, yet for some reason they always seem to fall short. How do you describe one of the most majestic and beautiful stretches of coastline in Ireland (maybe even the world!) in mere words and still do it justice?

I'm in my mid thirties now, and yet I still have vivid memories as a child going on family holidays to Portrush. Whether it was fishing in rockpools, running up and down the sand dunes at the Whiterocks Beach or playing golf at Ballyreagh. And over twenty years later, the draw to visit the 'Causeway Coast' is still just as strong. As a landscape photographer, it provides hours and hours of endless photographic opportunities, especially if you veer away from the 'tourist hot spots'. As a husband and father, it gives me many reasons to jump in the car and go exploring on family days out to make new memories of our own.

Even on a wet day, it draws me back. It's one of the few places I could go and visit with a smile on my face when the weather forecast is suggesting I stay indoors.

It fulfils a need for beauty and wide open spaces. For beaches, cliff paths and the sound of the ocean. Whether I'm out shooting the stillness of a sunrise, the wildness of an Atlantic storm or the awesomeness of an Aurora display. It's my 'go-to' place. Hopefully this book will inspire you to explore it too.

Where do you start on the Causeway Coast? By way of a short disclaimer, this is not a detailed guide to every must see spot along the Causeway Coast. Rather, this is my journey, as a photographer. This is the Causeway Coast I have grown up to love. This is the Causeway Coast I enjoy exploring. Yes, we'll visit the well know places (after all, how could we leave them out?) but hopefully many of the photos you see will be from places that you may not recognise. If that is case, then I've done my job.

The Berrins Fishery, Portstewart, Co. Londonderry

Portstewart Strand, Co. Londonderry

Portstewart Strand, Co. Londonderry

Opposite: **Dunluce Castle, Co. Antrim**
This is the biggest and probably most well-known castle along the Causeway Coast. The castle was first built by the MacQuillan family somewhere around 1500 but was seized by the MacDonnell clan in the 1550s. The castle is steeped in many myths and tales, one being the story of a banshee that is said to haunt the ruins. Another legend states that part of the kitchen closest to the cliff face fell into the sea, with only a kitchen boy surviving. The castle served as the seat of the Earl of Antrim until 1690. It is also rumoured to have been the inspiration for Cair Paravel in C.S. Lewis' Chronicles of Narnia.

THE CAUSEWAY COAST

Larrybane, Co. Antrim
The view from just below the disused quarry at Larrybane, looking back across Boheeshane Bay towards Ballintoy Harbour. Many years of blasting in the quarry made the surrounding cliff area prone to rock falls. The ruins of this quarry and the headland itself are easily accessed either via the coastal cliff walk from Ballintoy or by parking at the Rope Bridge.

THE CAUSEWAY COAST

Downhill Beach, Co. Londonderry
People often make the mistake of thinking that beach walks need be reserved for those beautiful sunny summer evenings. Needless to say, that's not the case. This is one of my favourite photos from Downhill Beach, a location I often shoot at sunrise. Situated 'below' Mussenden Temple, the beach provides amazing views looking west towards the shores of Co. Donegal. Quite often conditions can change quite quickly as the rain and wind blows in off the Atlantic.

THE CAUSEWAY COAST

The Whiterocks, Portrush, Co. Antrim
A favourite amongst families enjoying a day out at the seaside, the Whiterocks Beach is probably one of the nicest beaches that the Causeway Coast has to offer. Combine this with the new cliff-top path that has recently opened, and you can enjoy breath-taking views looking east towards Dunluce Castle and the Giant's Causeway.

Opposite: **Fairhead, Murlough Bay, Co. Antrim**
To the east of Ballycastle sits a beautiful secluded bay known as Murlough Bay. It's quite a drive down into it and certainly not for the faint hearted. It provides amazing views of Rathlin Island on a clear day, but for me one of the things I love most about it is the profile of Fairhead it provides. If you hit it at the right time of year, you can also stumble across a great display of coastal bluebells.

THE CAUSEWAY COAST

Portstewart, Co. Londonderry
As much as we like to think we can predict the weather, quite often we have no idea what's about to happen. This particular evening I was on a commission for a particular shot that a client wanted, when I suddenly had to change plans in order to capture this amazing light display that just appeared out of nowhere. That's one of the intriguing things about the coast, the weather can change in an instant.

Opposite: **Whitepark Bay, Co. Antrim**
Nestled perfectly between Portbradden and Ballintoy is Whitepark Bay Beach. A much smaller and quieter beach than some of the others featured, Whitepark Bay is extremely popular and once you arrive there, you'll understand why. There is a great viewing area up above the beach just on the roadside, yet I think the real beauty here is to be had down at the water's edge. On days when the tide conditions are right, you can enjoy a beautiful walk from Portbradden all the way round to Ballintoy and beyond.

THE CAUSEWAY COAST

Portstewart Point, Co. Londonderry
Just to the west of the Herring Pond you will find Portstewart Point. I have to admit I wasn't overly enthusiastic about the location or the lighting on this particular evening, until this amazing heart-shaped cloud started to appear in the sky!

Portbradden, Co. Antrim
Sitting in its own little secluded corner of Whitepark Bay Beach is the tiny hamlet of Portbradden, which derives its name from the Irish 'Port Bradan' meaning 'port of the salmon'. It used to be home to Ireland's smallest church, St Gobban's, which was built back in the 1950s and was only 11ft 4in by 6ft 9in in size. I've enjoyed many a summer's sunset looking back towards Portbradden from the beach at Whitepark Bay.

THE CAUSEWAY COAST

Downhill beach, Co. Londonderry
A favourite amongst horse riders and fishermen, Downhill Beach provides an alternative view of Mussenden Temple which sits precariously on the cliff edge above. These shots were taken on the same morning, one before sunrise and the others just after. If you time it right, you may also catch the train before it disappears into the cliff below the Temple. Another great location that has featured in *Game of Thrones*.

Murlough Bay, Co. Antrim
Probably one of the most photographed trees on the whole of the north coast and it's quite obvious why. Murlough is a fantastic location to visit in the very early morning and if you arrive well before dawn, prepare yourself as you could stand a good chance of seeing some of the wild deer that come down from the hills before sunrise.

THE CAUSEWAY COAST

Whiterocks Beach, Co. Antrim
A beautiful location to watch the sun coming up in the midst of the summer months. I had almost perfect conditions on this particular morning. I always had a shot in mind of the Whiterocks at sunrise and high tide. Thankfully this particular morning, the early start paid off. From the beach or the cliff path walk, you can enjoy amazing views of these limestone cliffs and the distinguishable headlands of Shelagh's Head, the Wishing Arch, Elephant Rock and the Lion's Paw.

THE CAUSEWAY COAST

This page & opposite: **The Giant's Causeway, Co. Antrim** Probably the most iconic, well known and most photographed location along the Causeway Coast. The Giant's Causeway is a 'must visit' on anyone's itinerary. These world-famous polygonal basalt columns are steeped in myth and legend. The Giant's Causeway is a UNESCO World Heritage Site and was awarded the UK's Best Heritage Attraction in 2015 at the British Travel Awards. Some say it was the mighty Irish giant, Finn McCool, who carved this area in a fight against the Scottish giant, Benandonner (The Red Man).

Portcoon, The Giant's Causeway, Co. Antrim
A short ten-minute cliff walk west of the Giant's Causeway Visitor Centre is the secluded little cove known as Portcoon. Surrounded by huge cliffs on either side, this cove is definitely worth a visit. A hidden gem which many overlook. One of my favourite times to visit is during high tide – it's quite an experience to witness the huge swells come crashing in!

Port Watty, Ballycastle, Co. Antrim

The unmistakable outline of Fairhead lurking in the distance as the sun appears above the horizon. A 3:00am start is a regular occurrence during our summer months to get up to the coast and into position for sunrise. I came across this spot one morning when I had intended to visit Pans Rock but had to improvise as the bridge was under repair. A short walk east along the shoreline led me here. On such a clear morning as this one, you can even make out the silhouette of Scotland away in the distance. People often ask me about the 'glassy' look to the water on a lot of my coastal photography. This isn't photoshopped, but rather it's created by using a long exposure and allowing the camera to record movement in the sea. On this particular morning it has created a very smooth glass-like effect that isn't visible to the naked eye.

THE CAUSEWAY COAST

Ballycastle and Rathlin Island
First light as it hits the shores of Ballycastle with Rathlin Island in the distance.

Pans Rocks, Ballycastle
Located at the eastern end of Ballycastle Beach, this outcrop of rocks provides a great viewpoint of Fairhead, Rathlin Island and the Scottish shoreline. This was taken before sunrise, when the sky was just about to waken, there was a nip in the air and hopes were high for the day ahead. I love the stillness of a dawn shoot. Quite often you have a location all to yourself, and you have time to reflect and relax. There's a stillness that you can't quite get at any other time of the day.

THE CAUSEWAY COAST

Downhill Beach, Co. Londonderry
You find yourself re-visiting certain locations time and time again in search of that elusive shot. This stretch of the coastline provides a landscape photographer with a unique opportunity, as it can be shot at both ends of the day. Here it is at dawn, with the lights of Portstewart still glimmering in the distance. The beach stretches 11km and provides amazing views of Co. Antrim, Co. Londonderry and Co. Donegal.

THE CAUSEWAY COAST

Dunseverick, Co. Antrim
As a 'sunset chaser' quite often I come home empty handed. Yet this evening at Dunseverick I seemed to strike it lucky. I used to think I could predict the outcome ahead of time, but I slowly began to realise that I couldn't because it was those evenings when you least expected it that would end up leaving you in utter disbelief. A bit like this particular evening. Just after sunset, out of nowhere, the sky just went on fire, as if someone had lit a match. Within a matter of minutes it had gone again, a fleeting moment in time never again to be repeated.

Opposite: **The Secret Beach, Ballintoy Harbour, Co. Antrim**
If you want to enjoy a little bit more privacy on the Causeway Coast, then the Secret Beach at Ballintoy is the place to go. A beautiful secluded little cove just below the harbour provides fantastic views of Sheep Island and Rathlin Island. The outcrop of rocks just out of shot to the left is popular with fishermen. This area has also featured in *Game of Thrones*.

THE CAUSEWAY COAST

THE CAUSEWAY COAST

THE CAUSEWAY COAST

**The Secret Beach,
Ballintoy Harbour, Co. Antrim**
The life ring perched on the rocks is a constant reminder of the dangers of the seas. I didn't get the sunrise I was hoping for on this particular morning, but instead was greeted with a very moody 'cold' looking image as the clouds streaked across the sky just after dawn.

THE CAUSEWAY COAST

Kinbane, Co. Antrim
Between Carrick-A-Rede Rope Bridge and Ballycastle lie the ruins of Kinbane Castle. The views from Kinbane Head are astonishing if you can brave the steep decline down the side of the cliff. Just nestled to the east of the castle ruins is an old fisherman's cottage. I arrived with plenty of time for sunrise, yet it was after the sun had risen that the magic happened this morning as the cliffs to the east basked in soft morning light, unveiling an array of sea caves dotted along the coastline.

Kinbane Castle, Co. Antrim
What's left of Kinbane gets silhouetted against the colours of the morning sky.

THE CAUSEWAY COAST

Kinbane Castle, Co. Antrim

THE CAUSEWAY COAST

Ballycastle Beach, Co. Antrim
A beautiful sunset sky taken from Ballycastle Beach looking back towards the town with the unmistakable outline of Kinbane Castle lurking on the horizon. Again, a long exposure has given the incoming tide a very calming and ethereal feel.

THE CAUSEWAY COAST

Left: **Elephant Rock, Ballintoy, Co. Antrim**
A short ten-minute walk round from Ballintoy Harbour and you'll come across a volcanic stack known to locals as 'Elephant Rock'. As you can see, there's really no need for an explanation as to how it got its name. At a certain time of the year, it's said that if you're in the right position, you can capture the sun beginning to set in the gap at the Elephant's trunk. Elephant Rock and the surrounding coves are links in a beautiful walk between Ballintoy Harbour and Whitepark Bay Beach (at low tide).

Opposite: **Ballintoy, Co. Antrim**
There's a lot to be said about the waters around this stretch of the Causeway Coast. At times, large sea swells can appear from nowhere and unfortunately have been the cause of many tragedies in the past. From this spot you have fantastic views looking towards Sheep Island and Larrybane. Between Sheep Island and Larrybane lies a treacherous reef, where in 1906 a Fleetwood trawler returning from Iceland ran aground. By using long exposure photography, the sea often turns into a smooth blur or mist and can give a very peaceful and tranquil look to a scene, yet it's always good to remember the reality of what lies beneath and the dangers it can present.

THE CAUSEWAY COAST

Ballycastle Beach, Co. Antrim
Located less than five minutes from Ballycastle town centre, the beach here stretches 1.2km from the Marina and Harbour at the western side right along to an area known as Pans Rock to the east. A perfect location to enjoy an evening walk in anticipation of sunset or a morning stroll with beautiful views looking east towards the dominant headland known as Fairhead. This evening I arrived just in time to witness the sky seemingly catch on fire. The land to the right is Rathlin Island with the lights of Ballycastle just about visible to the left.

Portstewart, Co. Londonderry
Just to the east of Portstewart Strand runs a beautiful coastal walk that stretches from the Strand right round to the Main Promenade (past the Berrins fishery house). This shot was taken on the outcrop of rocks just below St Patrick's Well which sits overlooking the Strand. This little section of coast provides an abundance of rock pools and coves to explore. It also furnishes fantastic views looking towards Mussenden Temple which you can see perched on the cliff top, and Co. Donegal in the distance.

Murlough Bay, Co. Antrim
Located a short drive from Ballycastle along the Torr Head scenic route lies Murlough Bay. One of the most attractive bays along the Causeway Coast, Murlough lies quietly in the shadow of Fair Head, a dominant headland perched at it's western end. Coal used to be mined and shipped from Murlough Bay, but now it lies as a hidden gem of our coastline. There are many ruins which were once the miners' houses. Although the drive down can be 'a little hairy', don't let that put you off. It's best to park the car and explore this area on foot.

Portstewart Strand, Co. Londonderry

Sometimes it's the simple things that catch your eye, especially when the light is beautiful. I've walked this beach many many times and rarely did I ever stop and photograph these posts. However, on this evening, the tide was high and the posts were completely surrounded by water. Using a long exposure has helped smooth out the texture of the water and help emphasise the tranquillity I experienced that evening. Sometimes less is more!

Portstewart Strand, Co. Londonderry

A beautiful array of soft pastel colours slide their way across the sky at dusk. A typical evening on the Causeway Coast? I'm not so sure, but when it happens, there's no where else I'd rather be. Portstewart Strand lies between Portstewart and the Barmouth which seperates the strand from Castlerock Beach. The strand is owned and managed by the National Trust and holds a Blue Flag award.

THE CAUSEWAY COAST

Downhill Mausoleum, Co. Londonderry
Within the grounds of Downhill Demesne lies this stunning mausoleum, built by Frederick Hervey, the 'Earl Bishop', and dedicated to his brother George, the 3rd Earl of Bristol, Lord Lieutenant of Ireland. An impressive site to witness during the day, but even nicer (in my opinion) to visit at night under the faint green glow of the Aurora Borealis. This whole area has become very popular with astro photographers and those chasing the Aurora. Not just for its views, but also because it provides you with some amazing dark skies when the moon is absent.

The Whiterocks Beach, Portrush, Co. Antrim
A summer sunrise at the Whiterocks Beach, with views looking east towards Lacada Point at the Causeway. I usually arrive to a sunrise location in the dark in plenty of time to choose my shooting location and get everything set up as quite often the colours appear in the sky before the sun rises. Around ten or fifteen minutes before the sun hit the horizon, I was witness to a beautiful purple and red and pink glow to the sky before it very quickly faded.

THE CAUSEWAY COAST

The Bowl, Whiterocks, Portrush, Co. Antrim
Quite a contrast from the last shot, this image was taken thirty minutes later and you can see the vast difference in light. I turned my attention west this time and tried to time my shot in between waves, allowing the incoming waves to fill the bowl with water, and then retreat back so I could still see the detail in the rocks. This is the view looking back towards the famous sand dunes and the Skerries (visible on the right hand side).

Portballintrae Harbour, Co. Antrim

Nestled between the village of Bushmills and the ruins of Dunluce Castle lies the quaint little coastal village of Portballintrae. Back in the 1600s the harbour served as a landing point for the village and the nearby Dunluce Castle. Dunluce quickly developed into a thriving location for goods, especially from Scotland. Still to this day, the harbour is home to many local fishermen. This is the view from the western side of the harbour, looking back east towards Bushfoot Strand and the Causeway headlands. As is very often the case with the weather on the Causeway Coast, hanging around fifteen minutes can make a huge difference. I almost gave up on this shot until suddenly the sky to my right started to clear just enough to let some beautiful rich colour through.

Elephant Rock, Ballintoy, Co. Antrim

When the tide is low enough, you can happily explore this unique area of coastline, including the beautiful limestone arch which sits quietly in the shadows of the Elephant. Located nearby is a cave which once revealed Iron Age artifacts and it's also possible to find the odd fossilized ammonite or brachiopod in this area too.

Downhill Beach,
Co. Londonderry

Portcoon, The Causeway, Co. Antrim

Storms storms storms! If you're brave enough, our coastline is a stunning place to witness the full force of Mother Nature's fury. With huge sea swells and high winds predicted, I knew there was only one place I wanted to be – Portcoon. When I see conditions like these, I often wonder in years gone by, how anyone would ever attempt to bring a boat in here! Again, a long exposure was used to create drama and movement in not only the sea, but also the clouds. I love the contrast between the solidness of the jetty and the chaos all around it.

The Port Path, Portstewart, Co. Londonderry
Allow yourself to be swept away with amazing panoramic views of Portstewart Strand, Castlerock Beach, Downhill and Co. Donegal. The Port Path is not only part of The Causeway Coast Way but also an integral part of the Ulster Way too. This section close to the Strand is quite flat and very accessible, with two beautiful coffee shops just a few moments apart, offering stunning views over the sea.

Opposite: **The Horsehoe, Ballintoy, Co. Antrim**
Just to the east of the entrance to Ballintoy Harbour lies 'The Horsehoe'. I'm not sure if it officially has this name or not, but it should! A perfect example of coastal sea erosion, this horseshoe sits facing north east and looks towards Sheep Island and Rathlin Island. It's very easily accessed from the harbour: just walk back up the road from the harbour and you will see the laneway down into the Secret Beach. Once there, follow the rocks out as far as you can and you can't miss it!

THE CAUSEWAY COAST

THE CAUSEWAY COAST

Castlerock Pier, Co. Londonderry
A short drive from Coleraine will bring you to the coastal village of Castlerock, well known for its beautiful beach and amazing links golf course. Right at the eastern end of the 1km long beach lies the Lower River Bann estuary known as the Barmouth. This estuary actually separates Castlerock Beach from Portstewart Strand. This shot was taken just after sunset during the 'blue hour'. Again, a long exposure has helped smooth out the water. On a late summer's evening, the walk out to the end of the Barmouth and back along the beach to the car is well worth it.

Islandforglass and Islandoo, Ballintoy, Co. Antrim

The Berrins Fishery, Portstewart, Co. Londonderry
When you have a love of photography and a love of the coast, you need to prepare yourself to be out and about in all weather conditions. I believe that this is one of the things that attracts me to the coast. There's always a raw unpredictability about it, even on a nice sunny day. On this particular afternoon, I had to retreat back five times to the shelter of the Fishery House walls to take cover from the wind and rain that were blowing in off the Atlantic (much to the amusement of those sitting in the warmth of the nearby coffee shop!). Conditions were tricky and I always act cautiously when I'm around the sea, but at times you need to stick with it and wait it out in order to get the shot. On the sixth attempt, I managed to grab two very quick shots before I was forced to retreat for the final time. But thankfully I got the shot I had hoped for. Incidently, the Berrins, also known as the Berne Salmon Fishery, was a shore fishing station owned by the O'Neill family and up until the 1960s, it acted as a draft net fishery.

THE CAUSEWAY COAST

Murlough Bay, Co. Antrim
A new day dawns at Murlough Bay on the Antrim coast. I often wonder about the lives of those who lived and worked here as there are constant reminders of the past dotted everywhere. It's no wonder that *Game Of Thrones* chose this as one of their filming locations.

Kinbane, Co. Antrim
A very rare occurrence of some nacreous clouds, also known as Mother of Pearl clouds, just after sunrise at Kinbane Head. These clouds are laced with vivid iridescent light from below the horizon. This little bay is just to the eastern side of the castle ruins. This was taken just after the infamous 'Storm Henry' which battered our shores for a few days in 2016.

Kinbane Castle, Co. Antrim

Are you willing to endure the seemingly endless number of steps to get down to the foot of the castle ruins? I think you should! This is a beautiful bay offering great views towards Rathlin Island and Scotland. During the Victorian era, the story goes that guides who worked at the Giant's Causeway would row here to collect 'spar' (a beautiful crystalized deposit) which they would then take back with them to sell to visitors to the Causeway stones.

THE CAUSEWAY COAST

Ballintoy, Co. Antrim
Would you believe me if I told you that this shot was taken in the middle of the day? It looks more like a moody night shot, such was the intensity of the impending rain and storm clouds. Perhaps for a lot of people, the thought of trying to shoot long exposures in this kind of weather seems absurd, however, I relish the challenge! When you pull it off, you can create some very dramatic images.

Ballintoy Harbour, Co. Antrim

Is this the nicest harbour along the Causeway Coast? Can I be biased and say yes? Ballintoy's profile has jumped through the roof, mostly due to the popularity and success of *Game Of Thrones*, which has used the harbour (and various other stretches of the surrounding coastline) in much of their filming. In the summer months, this is still a busy little fishing harbour, yet in the 'off' season, it's not unusual for the harbour to lie empty. Conditions were tough whilst trying to shoot this image, battling the wind and lots of sea spray. But just as I was about to give up, a rainbow began to appear, which gave me the incentive to keep shooting, and I'm very glad I did.

Previous double page spread:

Ballintoy Parish Church, Co. Antrim

Ballintoy means 'town of the north' and the Ballintoy parish church is one of the most northerly in the diocese of Connor. The current building is said to date back to 1813, although there was an older structure here before the present one. Some of the most celebrated treasures held by the parish are a communion plate and paten made from solid silver, presented in 1684 by Sara Stewart of Ballintoy Castle. This is another fantastic location from which to view the Milky Way.

Left: **Downhill House, Downhill Demesne, Co. Londonderry**

I would have loved to have seen Downhill House in all its glory. Unfortunately disaster struck in May of 1851 when a fire almost completely gutted the house. Over 20 pieces of sculpture were ruined and even though the library was completely destroyed, most of the paintings were rescued. The house is characterised by a three storey front. What remains is a far cry from its former splendour.

**Mussenden Temple,
Co. Londonderry**
Under the night sky on this particular occasion, the temple almost looks like it's made from copper.

**Ballintoy Harbour,
Co. Antrim**
What could be nicer than this quaint little harbour lit by moonlight? Well, how about we add a feisty Aurora display to the mix? When conditions are right, we manage several Aurora displays along the Causeway Coast in the course of a year – some better than others. On this occasion, the Aurora was strong, and even with a bright moon, was still visible on camera. Ballintoy has become an extremely popular spot amongst 'Aurora hunters'. Sometimes when it's strong enough, it is visible to the naked eye. Yet on this occasion I had to rely on a long exposure to pull out all the colour in the night sky.

Elephant Rock, Co. Antrim
If you didn't see the stars, you could almost mistake this for a shot of the sun, yet this was taken in the middle of the night, lit solely by moonlight. In the right conditions, this is a beautiful area to explore, not just during the daytime, but also under the night sky.

Torr Head, Co. Antrim
On the headland itself sits the ruins of what used to be a signalling station. This lookout station would record the passage of transatlantic ships and relay the information and data back to Lloyds of London and the incoming destination port. Sometimes, shooting a sunrise isn't all about watching the sun 'rise' above the horizon. Quite often, it's about where this beautiful soft light lands, and this image is a perfect example. This is the view looking east from Torr Head towards Portaleen Salmon Fishery with Crockan Point and Runabay Head in the distance. The tides around Torr Head can be treacherous, even on a calm day. Torr Head is also a very popular spot amongst fishermen.

THE CAUSEWAY COAST

THE CAUSEWAY COAST

The Secret Beach, Ballintoy, Co. Antrim

Opposite: **Torr Head, Co Antrim**
Sunsets are nice. There's no doubt about it. But there's something special about rising early in the morning before sunrise, whilst everyone else is still in bed. Most of the time you have the coast to yourself. The drive to Torr Head in the dark isn't for the faint hearted. Known as one of the most scenic drives along the Causeway Coast, the Torr Head Scenic Route runs between Ballycastle and Cushenden and peaks at Torr Head, providing breath-taking views of the Mull of Kintyre and across the North Channel towards Scotland.

THE CAUSEWAY COAST

Portbraddan, Co. Antrim
If I had to give this image a name, I'd call it 'The Cauldron'. I headed to Portbraddan one morning for sunrise and stumbled upon this amazing little inlet which was taking quite a battering from the high tide. The waves kept crashing in and filling up the hollow 'cauldron' in the foreground rocks. The water would quickly drain away before the next wave hit. All of a sudden the sky lit up and this vibrant red only lasted a few minutes before it disappeared. Right place at just the right time I guess.

Kinbane Headland, Co. Antrim

Aurora + Milky Way + 'Selfie' makes for a happy photographer! Kinbane has become one of my favourite spots to photograph the night sky. It works especially well for shots of the Milky Way and the Aurora, and if you time it right, you can get both in the one shot! The Aurora was putting on a great display on this particular March night. Taken just before midnight, I decided to shoot the image from the cliff edge, about ¼ of the way down the steps. I wanted to ensure that the remains of the castle lay just below the horizon line and so I knew that a lower viewpoint wouldn't work. In order to get down and out onto the very edge of the castle headland, I set up the camera on the intervalometer which mean't it was going to be taking a twenty-five second exposure every thirty seconds. This allowed me the time I needed to scramble down the steps, across the rocks and out onto the headland to 'pose' in the shot. The beam is simply my headtorch pointed up into the night sky. I have to admit though, when it's dark and windy, you can feel a little exposed standing out on the edge of a headland trying to stay perfectly still whilst gazing up to the sky, listening to the waves crashing around the rocks below you!

Ballintoy, Co. Antrim

One of the nicest views along the Causeway Coast at dawn. Normally, this whole area is very easily accessed, except on mornings like this when there is a huge high tide and very rough seas. The simple change in tide can completely alter the look of any location, especially here. In the distance, you can make out the 30m high Ulster limestone cliffs of Larrybane Bay. Riddled with caves, especially on its western end, the bay has one prominent and unusual cave in the middle of it which is guarded by three massive tufa pillars.

The Giant's Causeway, Co. Antrim
A very prominent headland along the Causeway Coast, the main 'peak' above the Causeway stones is quite a sight to behold, especially when it is bathed in the early morning light. This photo taught me a very valuable lesson: always survey an area and look all around you. My initial plan was to shoot the 'stones' on this particular morning. I had been hoping for some nice morning side lighting as I waited patiently for the sun to rise above the main headland behind me. Then as soon as it did, I spotted the heart shaped cloud formation almost directly above the headland so I had to quickly adjust and managed to get the shot just before the cloud started to break apart. This location is probably one of the busiest along the Causeway Coast, and with good reason; however, on this morning, the early start meant I had the whole place to myself. Which made it even more special.

The Arcadia, Portrush, Co. Antrim
Probably one of the most iconic buildings in Portrush, this much-loved little bay proved a great spot for sunrise. Steeped in history, the Arcadia building was once a famous ballroom. It was built back in the 1920s and had been originally designed as a café, yet it opened its doors as a ballroom in 1953. It sits nestled between the East Strand and Portrush Main Street and is very easily accessed. From the bay itself, you have great views looking out towards The Skerries and the Whiterocks Beach. On a clear day, you can even make out the famous Giant's Causeway headlands far in the distance.

THE CAUSEWAY COAST

The Blue Pool, Portrush, Co. Antrim

Dunseverick Harbour, Co. Antrim
Storm Henry hit our province hard, and the Causeway Coast was especially affected. But whilst most sensible people were heading for cover, I was driving to Dunseverick in search of some epic seascapes. Huge sea swells, high tides and gale force winds made capturing this image extremely difficult. But I persevered and I'm glad I did. You can just about make out the outline of the harbour walls that are normally visible, which shows you how huge the sea swells were that day. This was shot from slightly above the harbour itself, looking north west towards The Sandy Ope and Geeragh Point, with the unmistakable Causeway headlands of Bengore and Benbane in the distance.

THE CAUSEWAY COAST

Downhill Beach, Co. Londonderry
When the tide is out at Downhill, it reveals a huge sandy beach full of amazing details to not only explore but also photograph.

Ballintoy, Co. Antrim
Morning light at Ballintoy, this time looking across Boheeshane Bay towards Carrick-A-Rede Rope Bridge with the impressive Sheep Island to the left. Boheeshane Bay is a popular spot amongst sea kayakers and divers.

Sheep Island, Co. Antrim
Located approx. 0.5km off the coast, Sheep Island has been named a Special Protection Area and An Area Of Special Scientific Interest. An early morning sunrise trip to photograph the limestone cliffs of Larrybane proved fruitless, until I turned and spotted this dramatic cloud formation forming over Sheep Island. Moments later, these clouds dumped a massive hail shower on us and we had to retreat and take shelter at the disused quarry. But not before the rising sun provided some magical side lighting and colours on the clouds.

Sheep Island, Co. Antrim
Another massive storm cell looming over Sheep Island, shot from the edge of the disused Larrybane Quarry.

Boheeshane Bay, Co. Antrim
There is an amazing cliff walk between Ballintoy and Carrick-A-Rede Rope Bridge which takes you along the top of Boheeshane Bay and Larrybane Bay. Around half way along Boheeshane Bay provides you with amazing views back towards Ballintoy Harbour. In landscape photography, so many elements need to come together and I think they all did on this particular morning as I setup my shot, trying to emphasise the parish church of Ballintoy in the distance, which was then perfectly complemented by a tiny rainbow in amongst the storm clouds.

Ballycastle Beach, Co. Antrim
Last light on Ballycastle beach, looking towards Rathlin Island and Pans Rock. You can also just about make out the headland of Kinbane Castle on the extreme left.

Ballycastle Beach, Co. Antrim
Dusk on Ballycastle Beach. Long exposures not only produce a nice ethereal effect on the water, but also can create some amazing streaks in the clouds, providing they are moving fast enough in the right direction!

THE CAUSEWAY COAST

Portbradden, Co. Antrim
Located on the western end of Whitepark Bay, Portbradden provides a great starting point for two very differing coastal walks, either towards Whitepark Bay Beach (when the tide is out) to the east or towards Dunseverick to the west via Gid Point, Portninish and Portacallan. This is the view looking back towards Gid Point at dawn. The scene was completely dark to my naked eye, yet the camera has captured some amazing colours which I couldn't see thanks to an extremely long exposure of several minutes.

THE CAUSEWAY COAST

Whitepark Bay / Dundriff Headlands, Co. Antrim
Amazing light hitting the Dundriff headlands looking back towards the eastern end of Whitepark Bay Beach. This spot sits nicely at the very edge of Whitepark Bay Beach and is also only a ten or fifteen minute walk from Ballintoy Harbour.

THE CAUSEWAY COAST

Strand Head, Portstewart, Co. Londonderry
Sunset taken on the rocks just below Strand Head, at the eastern end of Portstewart Strand.

Overleaf: **Portstewart Strand, Co. Londonderry**
Twightlight colours on Portstewart Strand.

Ballintoy Harbour, Co. Antrim
A lone boat bobs in the safety of Ballintoy Harbour at dawn. This is a slightly different viewpoint of the harbour, with the Scottish islands of Isla and Jura just about visible on the horizon. It's very rare to see the harbour car park empty!

Leckilroy Cove, Co. Antrim
Between Bushfoot Strand (at Portballintrae) and the Giant's Causeway lies a beautiful cliff walk which takes you along the headland at Runkerry and along past Portcoon towards the main Giant's Causeway Visitor Centre. The views along this stretch of cliffs are phenomenal. From here you can enjoy views right across the 'main' Causeway, towards the Chimney Tops at the far end of Port Noffer. For access, this spot is probably better reached from the Visitor Centre, but instead of venturing down towards the Causeway stones, you head along the cliff top to the west, past the back of the Causeway Hotel.

THE CAUSEWAY COAST

Elephant Rock and Long Gilbert, Ballintoy, Co. Antrim
The unmistakable outline of the Elephant stands silhouetted against the setting sun as I look out towards Long Gilbert.

Leckilroy Cove, Co. Antrim
The morning sun appears above the Great Stookan and the Chimney Tops at the Giant's Causeway.

Portcoon Headland, Co. Antrim

The view west towards Leckilroy Cove from the headland just above Portcoon. Much of the Causeway Coast is covered in this amazing sea pink (also known as 'thrift') from the end of spring until summer.

THE CAUSEWAY COAST

Leckilroy Cove, Co. Antrim
Soft evening light gently catches the sea pink along the cliff edges overlooking Leckilroy Cove and Portcoon.

Mussenden Temple, Co. Londonderry

Built in 1785 by Frederick Augustus Hervey, the Bishop of Derry and Earl of Bristol, the Temple forms part of the Downhill Demesne. It sits perched on the very edge of the 120ft cliff and was built as a summer library, dedicated to the memory of Hervey's cousin Frideswide Mussenden. As well as being one of the most photographed spots along the Causeway Coast, the Temple is also popular for civil wedding ceremonies.

THE CAUSEWAY COAST

Carrick-A-Rede Rope Bridge, Co. Antrim

First erected by salmon fishermen in 1755, Carrick-A-Rede Rope Bridge joins the mainland to the tiny island of Carrick-A-Rede which is home to just one tiny building – a fisherman's cottage! The rope bridge is suspended almost 100 feet above the sea level and the bridge itself spans approximately 20 metres and is not for the fainthearted. The name Carrick-A-Rede means 'rock of the casting'. Back in the 1970s, the bridge had only one handrail and large gaps between the slats! Thankfully the current bridge is much safer although there have been reports of people not being able to face the walk back across and having to be rescued from the island by boat. The island itself is a great example of a volcanic plug.

THE CAUSEWAY COAST

The Port Path, Strand Head, Co. Londonderry
Just east of Strand Head and the entrance onto Portstewart Strand lies another little secluded sandy bay with loads of little rock pools to be explored.

Opposite: **Portaneevey, Carrick-A-Rede, Co. Antrim**
The stretch of coastline between the Rope Bridge at Carrick-A-Rede and Ravens Point (also known as Gobe Feagh) is best enjoyed first thing in the morning. This is the view that greets you from the Rope Bridge looking east. You can even make out the beautiful outline of Fair Head in the distance.

The Port Path, Portstewart, Co. Londonderry
Sunset from another little cove along the Port Path, this time a little closer to the Berrins Fishery.

The Great Stookan, The Giant's Causeway, Co. Antrim
This is the view overlooking Portnaboe from the top of the Great Stookan headland. This viewpoint provides amazing views both east and west. Portnaboe, also known as 'Port of the Cow', contains the remains of what looks like low stone walls, which some people believe were built by the Vikings for shelter when they raided the Causeway. Who really knows?

THE CAUSEWAY COAST

THE CAUSEWAY COAST

Whitepark Bay Beach, Co. Antrim

Opposite: **Port Granny, The Giant's Causeway, Co. Antrim**
Looking back east from the top of the Great Stookan headland, you'll enjoy amazing views over Port Granny and Port Noffer which are separated by the famous Causeway stones. There are two walks available along this stretch of coastline, one along the water's edge and the other along the cliff edge. The stretch of coastline from the Great Stookan to the Causeway stones used to be popular with local traders who would try and sell visitors their handmade crafts. Legend has it that it used to be illegal to sell alcohol here so the 'older' ladies used to sell water in a glass and then poured in the alcohol 'for free'. Whether this is true or not I'm not sure, but if it is, then fair play to them!

THE CAUSEWAY COAST

Portmoon Bothy, Co. Antrim
Part of the Causeway Coast cliff path, Portmoon is best accessed from the Dunseverick side where parking is available at the side of Dunseverick Castle. The Portmoon bothy is a popular spot amongst sea kayakers who need somewhere to shelter for an overnight stay. Capable of holding six people, this little bothy provides a very unique experience for visitors enjoying the Causeway Coast.

THE CAUSEWAY COAST

Portnagovna, Dunseverick, Co. Antrim
Early morning sea mist rolls in obscuring Ballintoy and Whitepark Bay. Another amazing view looking back across Portnagovna, Portnahooagh and Horse Garrick from the cliff walk just east of Portmoon.

THE CAUSEWAY COAST

Port Reostan, The Giant's Causeway, Co. Antrim
A fellow photographer and good friend enjoying the sunset high up on the Causeway cliffs, overlooking Port Reostan and Spaniard Rock. This little bay is home to the Amphitheatre and the Chimney Stacks. You can also just about make out the remains of a lower path which has now been closed due to rockfalls.

Benanouran Head, The Causeway, Co. Antrim

The view back towards Hamilton's Seat taking in Port Na Tober and the Giant's Eye Glass. The large sea arch which once resembled a glass monacle has now collapsed into the sea making it a little more difficult to identify the Eye Glass. But what a view nonetheless! Because most of this cliff path is pretty exposed, especially the section at this spot, extra care needs to be taken when venturing along here.

Portmoon Bay & Bothy, Co. Antrim

THE CAUSEWAY COAST

Hamilton's Seat, The Causeway, Co. Antrim

Is this the best cliff top view along the Causeway Coast? I'm not sure, but I know it's definitely one of my favourites for sure. This is taken from Hamilton's Seat looking back west towards the main Causeway and is roughly halfway between the Giant's Causeway Visitor Centre and the parking facilities at Dunseverick Castle. Again, this is an extremely exposed section of the cliff walk, yet it offers some of the most staggering views of this rugged coastline. From here, you have fantastic views of Horseshoe Harbour, Port Na Tober, Benanouran Head, Port Na Spaniagh and Lacada Point.

THE CAUSEWAY COAST

Portmoon and Benadanir, Co. Antrim
I managed to get this shot by following what looked like a narrow sheep track part of the way down the cliff face. I was almost directly above the Portmoon Bothy which is just out of shot.

THE CAUSEWAY COAST

Port Noffer, The Giant's Causeway, Co. Antrim
By following the cliff path from the Visitor Centre, you will eventually arrive at the Port Reostan headland which provides awesome views back across Port Noffer and Port Granny, separated by the main Causeway stones. The Great Stookan headland is also clearly visible from here too.

THE CAUSEWAY COAST

Port Granny and The Great Stookan, The Giant's Causeway, Co. Antrim
Angry storm clouds and fork lightning battered the Causeway Coast as I made my way back to the safety of the car. I was round at Lacada Point when weather conditions took a turn for the worst so I made my way back along the cliff path, but I had to stop and fire off a few shots as the lightning lit up the night sky!

Carrick-A-Rede, Co. Antrim

I think this particular morning will stick in my memory for a lifetime. My original plan was to drive to Carrick-A-Rede for a sunrise shoot but I was running late due to traffic and as I was approaching the coast I noticed the sky was beginning to light up with some beautiful pastel colours. I decided to scrap my original plan and head to Ballintoy Harbour as this was my closest spot and I was scared of missing the colours. However, when I setup at Ballintoy, I couldn't settle and was getting frustrated as I couldn't get a fresh or original composition. So I decided to gamble and head back to the car and try and make it round to the Rope Bridge before the sun came up. When I arrived at the car park, I could see all this fog and mist rolling down off the cliff edge, but I still had a good fifteen minute walk/sprint to get down to the Rope Bridge. Thankfully I did and I was totally in awe of the scene that was unfolding before me. The mist and fog were rolling off the cliffs and down onto the sea like a river, and continued to do so for a good twenty minutes or more. I was mesmerised! But the icing on the cake for me was that I had the whole place to myself and I was the only one to witness this amazing display of nature.

THE CAUSEWAY COAST

Elephant Rock, Co. Antrim

Magheracross Headland, Portrush, Co. Antrim
These white limestone cliffs stretch from Curran Strand right along to Dunluce Castle and are riddled with a multitude of caves and arches. Some of these headlands have been given very unique names, such as Elephant Rock, the Lion's Paw, the Wishing Arch and Shelagh's Head. Many of the caves along this section of coastline actually stretch inland underneath the main road.

THE CAUSEWAY COAST

Portmoon Bothy, Co. Antrim
The rising sun dances across the ocean lighting some of the beautiful headlands between Portmoon and Dunseverick.

Opposite: **The Giant's Causeway, Co. Antrim**
The main headland behind the Causeway stones gets silhouetted against the night sky as the Milky Way core rises above Port Granny. For anyone hoping to catch a glimpse of the Milky Way core from these famous stones, a good time to visit is August or September, when skies are clear and the moon is hidden. The colours visible just under the core are the result of light pollution from Bushmills and Portballintrae but could almost be mistaken for the hues of the setting sun.

The Giant's Gate, The Giant's Causeway, Co. Antrim

It's one thing to explore the Grand Causeway in daylight and quite another to explore it in the dark, with just the stars to guide your way! Here we have the Giant's Gate with the Milky Way arching above it into the night sky. The Giant's Gate seperates Port Granny from Port Noffer and is part of the Grand Causeway.

Mussenden Temple, Co. Londonderry
A beautiful display of the Northern Lights (also known as the Aurora Borealis) dances across the sky behind Mussenden Temple. Although on this particular night the Lights were only slightly visible to the naked eye, an exposure of over twenty seconds has picked up a range of colours and formation and structure in the Aurora that I couldn't see.

THE CAUSEWAY COAST

Spaniard Rock and The Chimney Tops, The Giant's Causeway, Co. Antrim
Evening light on Spaniard Rock as viewed from the top of the Port Reostan headland.

THE CAUSEWAY COAST

Port Noffer, The Giant's Causeway, Co. Antrim
From this vantage point at Port Reostan, you have amazing views across the Grand Causeway, Port Noffer, Port Granny and the Great Stookan. You can also usually make out all the tourists and visitors to the main Causeway stones (called the Grand Causeway).

The Grand Causeway, The Giant's Causeway, Co. Antrim
Here we have a massive panorama taken on the Grand Causeway, with Spaniard Rock and Lacada Point on the extreme left and the Great Stookan on the extreme right. Around August / September time you can manage to capture the Milky Way arch across the sky above the Causeway headlands. It took several attempts to get this image right as there are so many elements that need to come together such as a very low tide, clear skies with zero cloud cover and no moon. There's something very special about standing on these stones surrounded by the ocean and looking up into the night sky and seeing our galaxy clearly visible to the naked eye. Amazing. The Milky Way is made up of over 100 billion stars and is so big that it takes light 100,000 years to cross from one side to the other.

Opposite: **Mussenden Temple and Downhill Demesne, Co Londonderry**
Shooting our stunning coastline under the night sky intrigues and excites me just as much as shooting it in normal daylight hours. Our night sky is alive! Two of my favourite things to shoot in the night sky are the Milky Way and the Aurora Borealis, but when you capture them both together, then that's even more special!

THE CAUSEWAY COAST

Ballintoy Harbour, Co. Antrim
One of the most popular spots for anyone chasing the Aurora along the Causeway Coast is Ballintoy Harbour. On this occasion I was fortunate enough to arrive just in time to capture quite a number of pillars in the display, which doesn't always happen. I had hoped for a great night shooting the Aurora as the skies were to remain clear, however, within about ten minutes the display died down and it never started again! That's the thrill and frustration of the Aurora hunt I guess.

THE CAUSEWAY COAST

Kinbane Head, Co. Antrim
A very faint Aurora display makes an appearance at Kinbane Head. I also happened to capture my first iridium flare (top right) in the night sky. Of the 3000 spacecraft currently in the earth's orbit, approximately 100 of them are Iridium Communications spacecraft. The glare from one of these satellites is known as an iridium flare.

THE CAUSEWAY COAST

Left: **The Lion's Gate, Downhill Demesne, Co. Londonderry**
This used to be the main entrance to Downhill Demesne and Mussenden Temple but was later replaced by the Bishop's Gate. The gate is guarded by two heraldic ounces or snow leopards which are the supporters of the Hervey coat of arms. At just the right time of the year, you can manage to get the Milky Way core rise between these two 'creatures'.

Opposite, top: **Ballintoy Parish Church, Co. Antrim**
The key to a good star trail image is making sure that Polaris (the North Star) is in the frame! A good way to find the North Star is to look for the Big Dipper, as Polaris is the last star on its handle. There are several fantastic phone Apps that will help with this – all you have to do is point them at the night sky and they will tell you what you are looking at. This image took just over an hour to take, so it's obviously important to have clear skies as any cloud cover would completely ruin your shot.

Opposite, bottom: **Ballintoy Parish Church, Co. Antrim**
An astro shot with not just the Milky Way core visible but also the International Space Station. Here it is heading towards the Milky Way as it travels across our night sky at a speed of roughly 17,150 mph. It's the size of a football field and is the third brightest object in our night sky, so it's very easy to recognise. In this shot, the streak you see is the distance the ISS travelled during a twenty-five second exposure!

THE CAUSEWAY COAST

The Herring Pond, Co. Londonderry
Just to the west of Portmore and the Blowing Hole, lies the Herring Pond. This is a popular spot amongst bathers who love to enjoy the 'freshness' of the Atlantic!

Opposite: **Ballintoy Parish Church, Co. Antrim**

THE CAUSEWAY COAST

Mussenden Temple, Co. Londonderry

Do you ever take the time to look up? At night, our skies are full of life, and yet most of us miss it. Here we have Mussenden Temple, sitting proudly under the Milky Way. Off to the left you can see the outline of Downhill House (which was gutted by fire in 1851) and to the right, the lights of Co. Donegal. For anyone wanting to explore and view the night sky, on a clear night, there's no better than place than the Downhill Demesne.

Lacada Point and The Chimney Tops, The Giant's Causeway, Co. Antrim
It was along this stretch of the Causeway Coast that the galleon of the Spanish Armada, *La Girona*, sank in 1588. A total of 1300 lives were sadly lost that night, with only nine sailors rumoured to have survived. *La Girona* had docked in Killybegs Harbour for repairs to her rudder and had taken crew on board from *La Rata Santa Maria Encoronada* and the *Duquesa Santa Ana*. On that fateful night of the 26 October, it was on its way to Scotland and was driven ashore at Lacada Point. It is said that 260 bodies were washed ashore.

THE CAUSEWAY COAST

Pans Rock, Ballycastle, Co. Antrim
Blue hour, looking back towards the coastal town of Ballycastle.

THE CAUSEWAY COAST

Dunseverick Falls, Dunseverick, Co. Antrim
There aren't too many waterfalls along our coastline that flow into the ocean and that are as easyily accessed as this one. A short walk from the ruins of Dunseverick Castle, this is best visited after a heavy rainfall and at low tide.

Runkerry Strand, Portballintrae, Co. Antrim

The tiny seaside village of Portballintrae is home to one of the best surfing beaches along the Causeway Coast, Runkerry Strand. It is located between Portrush and Bushmills and if you walk to the eastern end of the strand, you join the Causeway cliff path which twists its way around Runkerry Head towards the Causeway Visitor Centre. The beach is also known to locals as Salmon Rock Beach.

Salmon Rock Beach, Portballintrae, Co. Antrim

THE CAUSEWAY COAST

Runkerry Strand, Portballintrae, Co. Antrim
A lone pebble makes the perfect foreground interest for this sunset image from Portballintrae. In the distance is Cregganeagh, Salmon Rock and Murrial Point.

Portandoo Harbour, Portrush, Co. Antrim
The view from what remains of Portandoo Harbour, nestled between the Blue Pool and Ramore Head.

THE CAUSEWAY COAST

Portandoo Harbour, Portrush, Co. Antrim

Rinagree Point, Co. Londonderry
A beautiful section of coastline stretches between Portstewart and Portrush. It is riddled with coves and bays and a beautiful coastal path that joins these two seaside towns. This is Rinnagree Point, looking back across Stoney Port and Port Cool towards Portstewart.

Portandoo, Portrush, Co. Antrim
Storm clouds and rainbows fill the sky towards Reviggerly and the Skerries. Just another typical boisterous morning on the Causeway Coast.

Lansdowne Slipway, Portrush, Co. Antrim
What remains of the old lifeboat slipway beside Portandoo Harbour, which lies just round the corner from Ramore Head.

Rinagree Point, Co. Londonderry
Huge waves batter the coastline around Rinagree Point and Broad Isle on a late autumnal evening just after dusk. From this headland you have amazing views looking over Port Gallen and Sycamore Port towards Ballyreagh and Portrush.

Opposite: **The Skerries, Portrush, Co. Antrim**
Just off the coast of Portrush sits a beautiful group of tiny islands called the Skerries. They are a small group of rocky islands, popular with divers and are part of an Area of Special Scientific Interest. Many local boat trips leaving Portrush will pass these islands on their way to the Giant's Causeway. Back in 1879, the *Thomas Graham* sailing vessel was stranded and lost on these islands.

Stoney Port, Co. Londonderry
One of the best times to be out experiencing the coast is when the weather is changeable. The coastline takes on a whole new look and feel to it and I love shooting in this kind of weather.

THE CAUSEWAY COAST

Lansdowne Slipway, Portrush, Co. Antrim

Gid Point, Portbradden, Co. Antrim

There are many hidden little bays to explore around Gid Point, which sits just to the west of Portbradden. But take extra care so as not to be caught out by the tides around this section of coastline as you could easily find yourself stranded and having to find an alternative route back to your car.

Opposite: **Sea Gull Isle, The Giant's Causeway, Co. Antrim**

An exciting area of the Causeway to explore, Sea Gull Isle sits at the eastern end of Port Noffer, just beside Port Reostan.

THE CAUSEWAY COAST

THE CAUSEWAY COAST

Port Reostan and Lacada Point, Co. Antrim

Rathlin Island
A ferry runs across from Ballycastle to Rathlin Island on a daily basis. The island is L-shaped and is 6 miles long and 1 mile wide. Apart from the raw beauty of the place, a big attraction is the puffin season, which runs from April to July. There are many myths surrounding Rathlin, one of which I heard involved Robert the Bruce, the King of Scotland. Rumour has it that in 1306, the English King, Edward I, drove him out of Scotland and he had to take refuge on Rathlin. The story goes that he watched a spider persevering to bridge a gap in its web, and when it eventually succeeded, this gave him heart and he returned again to Scotland to take back his crown.

Portacallan, Co. Antrim

Easily accessed from Dunseverick Harbour, this is only a short walk from the car park behind the harbour. It can also be accessed from Portbradden when the tide is far enough out.